TRUTH

of the War Conspiracy of 1861

H. W. Johnstone

Foreword by Walter D. Kennedy and James R. Kennedy
Edited by Frank B. Powell, III

*"Everyone should do all in his power to collect
and disseminate the truth."* — *R.E. Lee*

December 3, 1865

REPRINTED BY

The
Scuppernong Press

Wake Forest, NC
www.scuppernongpress.com

Truth of the War Conspiracy of 1861
By H. W. Johnstone

Foreword by Walter D. Kennedy and James R. Kennedy
Biography by Charles Kelly Barrow
Edited by Frank B. Powell, III

©2012 The Scuppernong Press

First Printing

The Scuppernong Press
PO Box 1724
Wake Forest, NC 27588
www.scuppernongpress.com

Cover and book design by Frank B. Powell, III

International Standard Book Number
ISBN 978-1-9428063-4-9

Library of Congress Control Number: 2012949089

❧ Contents ❧

Ft. Sumter

❧ Foreword ❧

Lincoln's Conspiracy to Initiate the "Civil War"

Abraham Lincoln holds an almost god-like status in American history. President Ronald Reagan often cited or quoted Lincoln — President Barack Obama loves to compare his presidency to that of Lincoln's. Conservative talking heads universally bow before Father Abraham's altar and sing his praises while demonizing anyone so rash as to question Lincoln — the icon of modern America's "one nation indivisible."

Most patriotic Americans see the USA as a morally principled nation seeking to promote peace and freedom. But is this really the legacy established by Father Abraham? Could it be that the US, following the example set by Lincoln, is capable of initiating or promoting war for commercial advantage?

The Federal Empire's Post-Appomattox Colonial Expansion

After the defeat and occupation of the Confederate States of America in 1865 the Federal Empire was free to reduce Native American resistance in the American West. By the end of the nineteenth century most Native American lands had been seized and the inhabitants *reconstructed* via the reservation system. With the American continent *settled* the Empire cast its eyes even further westward — toward the nation of Hawaii.

The Kingdom of Hawaii was formed by native islanders as early as 1810. Its strategic location in the Pacific Ocean made it a target of early European colonialists, especially Spain, Russia, Great Britain and France. In an effort to resist colonial attempts to dominate the Hawaiian nation King David Kalakaua proposed an alliance with Japan and other nations suffering from colonial expansionism. New England *missionaries* had already established a company in Hawaii which would eventually become the Dole Food Company. American intentions were made clear in 1875 when the US demanded that the sovereign nation of Hawaii cede to the US control of Pearl Harbor, Ford Island and around five miles of coast line. In 1893 Americans and Europeans lead a revolt against the reigning Queen and demanded a new government which would eventually disenfranchise most native Hawaiians. During this revolt the USS *Boston* sent marines ashore to "protect" American interests. The landing of American troops helped to remove Hawaii's Queen and replace her with a government which would eventually be dominated by non-natives. After disenfranchising native Hawaiians a new government was established and Sanford Dole (cousin to James Dole founder of Dole Foods) became the nation's president. Hawaii was then annexed to the US in 1900 and Sanford was eventually appointed to a federal judgeship.

This pattern of New England *missionaries* agitating for federal intervention in the affairs of a sovereign nation, using high sounding principles as the excuse for war, all in order to protect or expand their commercial interests is not new to those who know the history of Lincoln's *civil war*. Perhaps this is why standard American history (best described as Yankee propaganda) labors so hard to prevent Americans from knowing the truth about Lincoln and the War for Southern Independence.

He Who Initiates War Typically Perceives Benefits from War

Empires, especially democratically ruled empires, love war. War allows democracies to do things to other peoples which would never have been allowed absent war — for example: carpet bombing of non-military civilian areas. War allows democracies to do things to its own people which would never have been tolerated absent war — for example: federal airport agents groping men, women and children. Politicians in democracies are well schooled in the technique of rattling war sabers in order to get patriotic Americans to rally-around-the-flag and protect the nation from real or perceived insults or threats. These patriotic Americans send their sons and daughters off to war to die for the expansion of the empire while being told that they are fighting a war to end all wars; to make the world safe for democracy; to save the Union, or some other high-sounding principle. In the end the common people pay a high price in blood, treasure, national debt, and loss of individual liberties, while the ruling class and those with close connections to the ruling class enjoy the benefits of their ill-gotten gains. Thus it has always been with empires — Lincoln's federal empire was and is no exception.

Why Would Lincoln Initiate a War?

What motive would Lincoln have to initiate a *civil war*? The old adage of "follow the money" provides the answer. As pointed out in *The South Was Right!* Northern newspapers were initially willing to accept the South's peaceful secession — viewing secession as an inherent right of a sovereign state under the Constitution. Indeed, New England states, during the War of 1812, threatened to secede from the Union. But by 1861 when Northern states began to count the potential cost of Southern secession — by way of loss tariff income from Southern ports — it quickly became a matter of ill-gotten gain vs. principles of constitutional government. Many Northern newspapers of the time were very clear about the need to protect northern interest in Southern resources. The *Union Democrat* in Manchester, New Hampshire, boldly proclaimed, "The Southern Confederacy will not employ our ships or buy our goods. ... It is clear that the South gains by this process, [secession] and we lose. NO — we MUST NOT let the South go." [Emphasis in the original]. The March 30, 1861, issue of *The New York Times* was equally clear, "With us it is no longer an abstract question — one of Constitutional power of the State or Federal Government, but of material existence and moral position both at home and abroad...We were divided and confused till our pockets were touched." The statement "till our pockets were touched" makes it clear the Northern states, led by Lincoln, viewed the South not as an equal partner in a constitutionally limited Republic of Republics but as a *cash cow*. Those in charge of the Federal Empire viewed the South as their property — a vast source of material wealth to be exploited by and for the benefit of those in control of the Federal Empire. In 1828 Senator Thomas Benton of Missouri declared the South provided more than 75 percent of the income needed to finance the federal government. To add insult to injury the majority of these federal dollars were spent on internal improvements benefiting Northern states and Northern commercial interests. Lincoln and Northern war governors would not allow their Union to lose such valuable resources. Added to this was the tremendous commercial boom a war economy would provide to the iron mills of Pennsylvania; the manufactures of New England, and windfall income generated for Northern railroads and financial interests on Wall Street. It is said that when Lincoln was asked why not just let the South go and avoid war, Lincoln proclaimed, "Let the South go? Let the South go! Where then shall we gain our revenues?" Empires depend on the exploitation of its colonial subjects to maintain and increase the wealth of the ruling elite and those with close (political and economic) connections to the empire's ruling elite. Thus, allowing the peaceful people of the South to enjoy a government ordered upon the consent of the governed would have forced the destruction of the emerging federal empire — and empires do not die easily.

Lincoln's *Civil War* to Protect and Defend the Empire Not the Constitution

The Constitution, Article II, Section 9, requires the president to be sworn into office by taking an oath to "… preserve, protect and defend the Constitution of the United States." Apologists for the Federal Empire (often referred to as educators — but in reality they are propagandists for the Federal Empire) have conditioned Americans to believe that preserving the Union is the same as "preserving the Constitution." Nothing could be further from the truth — in fact it is the exact opposite! Had Lincoln not initiated the War the Union would have remained but its geographical and political domain would have been reduced by some eleven to thirteen sovereign states. Lincoln initiated the *Civil War* not to preserve the constitutionally limited Republic of Republics as established by the founding fathers but to maintain and extend the domain of the Federal Empire!

Lincoln's Well-Kept Secret Conspiracy
to Invade a Sovereign Nation

Frank Powell, well known editor of the *Confederate Veteran* magazine, brings to our attention H. W. Johnstone's excellent work documenting Lincoln's successful efforts to force the South to defend itself and thereby appear to the Northern public as an aggressor. Lincoln's intent was to make the South appear as an aggressor which assaulted the US flag and national honor! Then Lincoln could rattle the war sabers and rally the people of the North to defend the flag. International law, acknowledged at the time, made it clear that if an aggressor nation (the USA in 1861) is threatening a peaceful nation (the CSA), the peaceful nation is within in its right to strike first in order to defend itself. The idea was that it is not necessarily the nation who strikes first who is the aggressor but the nation who makes the first strike necessary which must be branded as the aggressor. In *Truth of the War Conspiracy of 1861* Johnstone explains how Lincoln and his co-conspirators used deceit, half truths, lies and violation of international law to promote their war conspiracy. Johnstone wrote his book in 1917 using documentation which was not available when the post war Confederates, such as Davis, Stephens, Semmes and Pollard wrote their histories of the conflict. Johnstone adds even more documentation and explanation to how Lincoln managed to initiate his war of aggression against the people of the South who merely wanted to be "left alone" to live under a government ordered on the consent of the governed. Liberty and Empires cannot coexist — and Lincoln made sure the Federal Empire would be preserved.

Deo Vindice

James Ronald Kennedy
Walter Donald Kennedy
www.kennedytwins.com

Truth of the War Conspiracy of 1861

◈ Introduction ◈

H. W. Johnstone created quite a stir at the 1922 United Confederate Veterans Reunion in Richmond, Virginia, with the introduction of his pamphlet *Truth of the War Conspiracy of 1861*. While the convention unanimously recommended the pamphlet, there was immediate disapproval across the country by members of the press. This is not surprising to those of us living in the 21st century who have been indoctrinated by the myth of Saint Abraham our entire lives. But, Lincoln worship was already in place in 1922 and Johnstone's words were totally out of step with the mainstream media of the day.

Johnstone wrote his booklet after years of research and all of his statements are referenced, most of them coming from the pages of the *Official Records of the Union and Confederate Navies in the War of the Rebellion* — a publication of the United States government.

In the August 1922 issue of the *Confederate Veteran* magazine Johnstone states in a letter to the editor, "A very large percentage of current histories and biographies are loose compilations of opinions, very often regardless of facts as Henry Watterson said: 'A confusing din of opinion.' I have used only facts. I am aware that the comments and conclusions as set forth in this pamphlet are opinions, but modified by the facts stated as their basis.

"Briefly, the facts — of official record — are impregnable; and the facts so established, the conclusions as stated, are inevitable. For the first time, these facts are so published that all may understand them. With one exception — to my knowledge — every comment written into the daily press has been the work of those who never saw the book; yet they, and a very few equally ignorant individuals, denounced the United Confederate Veterans, the United Daughters of the Confederacy, the book and its author.

"There is a vast difference between 'before' and 'after' reading the truth. When the facts are refuted by openly produced evidence of equal dignity, I will publicly acknowledge it; but otherwise I stand to the truth, and bespeak the support of 'my kin folk.'"

Truth is the truth and Johnstone never had anyone to live up to his challenge. The truth just wouldn't support a challenge.

It was said at the time that it was a strong statement to assert any one man brought on the War For Southern Independence, but after reading *The Truth of the War Conspiracy* one can not help but come to this conclusion.

The Scuppernong Press is proud to republish this important work so it can again be on Southern and Northern bookshelves. It has been completely reset in a modern typeface with typos corrected and references checked for accuracy.

— Frank B. Powell, III, Editor
Wake Forest, North Carolina
August 2012

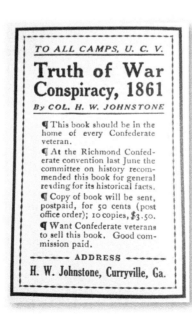

A Foreword

During President Washington's administration, at a banquet of the notables at Richmond, a young man, John Randolph of Roanoke, was called on for sentiment. Randolph arose, raised his glass, and said:

"George Washington, may he be damned" —

Instantly there was a howl of protest, a threatening movement. Randolph calmly waited; then continued —

— "If he signs Jay's Treaty!" —

There was a shout of approval.

I have somewhat to say.

Hear me through, then howl, or shout, as you may feel.

Memoranda

The crucial period in which the premeditated schemes of the fanatics were put into operations, so as to inaugurate actual war, was from March 4 to July 4, 1861; before Congress was allowed to meet, to consider it. From May 1861 to January 1862 I served in the "5th Georgia Volunteers," C.S.A. at Pensacola, Florida.

About July 1st, 1861, an expedition under our Colonel, John K. Jackson, attacked "Billy Wilson's Zouaves" (of Boston), on Santa Rosa Island, at night. We drove them — pell mell — into Fort Pickens; captured, and burned, their camps and immense stores. As we were returning to our boats we were attacked by a force of regulars of the U.S. Army. We drove them back; and my Captain, S. W. Mangham, captured their commanding officer, Major Vogdes, (who was mounted on a mule.)

Twenty years later, at Fort Adams, R.I., I met General Vogdes, who remembered the incident and discussed it. In his remarks he stated that *he had reinforced Fort Pickens before Fort Sumter was attacked; but, that his act was overshadowed by the clamor and furore about Fort Sumter.*

That was the first intimation I ever had of that fact. It

led me to search for some proof of it. I read Stephens, Davis, Semmes, Taylor, Maury, Shouier — and hundreds of authentic magazine articles — but none cleared the mystery enveloping that vital point. It was not until the records were opened to research — nearly twenty years later — that I found confirmation of Vogdes' statement, which led me through devious ways to other facts as to M. C. Meigs, H. A. Adams, J. L. Worden, D. D. Porter and many others.

The mystifying *dis* — arrangement of those records was a work of genius. It seems easy now, but I was years in getting the facts into chronological sequence.

In 1917 I succeeded in perfecting proofs fixing the responsibility for the War Between the States, 1861-1865, on one man — **Abraham Lincoln.**

My unconscious monitor, Vogdes, was one of the prisoners of war designated — by the Confederate War Department — to suffer the same fate as the Federal authorities threatened to execute on officers and men — (part of Admiral Semmes' command) — captured at the mouth of the Mississippi River in 1861. The *pirates* were not executed; so, Vogdes was saved.

One of the keenest observers I ever met was in Washington at the time of this secret War Conspiracy, Admiral Raphael Semmes, C.S.N. In 1870 a friend at Mobile invited me to accompany him to the "Anchorage," — the home of the Admiral — and for an hour I enjoyed the Admiral's reminiscences. As I left he said to me: "Captain, the secret treachery that caused the war will come to light, and justify the South. Truth is deathless!"

That was twenty-five years before the *secret* causes were unearthed; and then, were not comprehended, by the employees who handled them.

In the Encyclopedia Brittanica Lincoln's biographer (who sign S.F. and L.S.) says: "In early life Lincoln adopted these three maxims:

"1st. Never to swear;
"2nd. Never to touch liquor;

"3rd. Never to lie;
"And, he never did!"

I know nothing of his "swears."

I know Lamon and Herndon picture Lincoln waving a bottle in the midst of a drunken mob; and I remember, it was told, that he prescribed — "liquor like General Grant drinks!"

As to his "3rd maxim — Never to lie," I rest on the facts as will appear in this article.

From the same source I quote from Lincoln's first inaugural address, March 4th, 1861:

(B) "In your hands, my dissatisfied countrymen, and not in mine, is the momentous issue of civil war.

"The government will not assail you; you can have no conflict without being yourselves the aggressors."

That too — with his "3rd maxim" — I leave to be answered by the facts of record, as set forth in this article. Bear in mind that there was no *Civil War,* (except in Missouri); I am treating of the War Between the (Sovereign) States.

In this labor of many years, I have held frequent "imaginary conversations," discussions, arguments, with my loyal, trusted friend, the Blade — (my old service sword, which hangs on the wall, environed by books, records and memories.)

The Blade speaks for the *Truth*; and points to the record in this paper. I bespeak for my trusty friend your patience.

A word as to the spirit in which this paper is prepared.

If this article expresses my belief, it is because it sustains it. Abraham Lincoln is, to me, exactly what his own record makes him. It would be the same were the Prince of Peace the actor.

I served four years in the War between the States. I know what it is to meet men armed with a torch in one hand, the sword of diabolism in the other, (All were not so, else all would have died.) I know somewhat of the inferno of Reconstruction. I saw my people suffer, my father's house vandalized, my mother's tomb desecrated, I saw the South desolate!

Then, I saw my people rise; and, with a courage unequaled, restore our waste places and force a re-entrance to

"Our Father's house, to stay, thank God!"

My intent is to discover the facts, establish the Truth, as to the responsibility for the horrors of that war.

To attempt to describe such a tragic drama in cold, philosophic terms, would be to fail. If the acts be not set forth in words which portray their infamy it might be false, instead of an historical Truth.

Truth is not slander; nor partisan.

So, if a just indignation finds vent in good old English, occasionally, remember the South's 60 years of foul wrongs; and, if your view is worth notice, you will at least smile — as I do — my task being accomplished.

Map of Charleston Harbor

Truth of War Conspiracy
1861

When Washington was made president there was no party-line. John Adams succeeded him in 1797 without any definite party cleavage; but the laws passed under Adams' administration — by Hamilton's influence — aroused Thomas Jefferson and James Madison, who wrote into the Resolutions of 1798-9 "the first clear definite platform of Republican-Democratic principles;" which, supplemented by "Madison's Report," and epitomized in Jefferson's first inaugural address, set forth the basic principles of true Democracy.

The people rallied to them. Hamilton's Federalism was condemned and Jeffersonian Democracy voted into power.

It is interesting to recall that the first political struggle in Virginia, after these Resolutions were promulgated, was led by Jefferson's young kinsman, John Randolph of Roanoke, then 26 years old, and his first contest for office. He was opposed by the influence of Washington, Marshall and even Patrick Henry was somehow against him; but Randolph was elected, 1799, and became a powerful Democratic leader.

May I ask a pertinent question?

How long since you read those "Resolutions," or "Madison's Report," or Jefferson's first "Inaugural," or Calhoun's "Resolutions of 1833 and 7," or Jefferson Davis' "Resolutions" in the U.S. Senate in 1860?

If you are ignorant of them, how do you know what you believe; or that you are a Democrat?

There was never a truer patriot in America than John Adams; yet his administration caused his personal friend, Jefferson, to write the following in the noted Kentucky Resolutions.

Hark ye, the father of Democracy speaks:

(A) "This Commonwealth is determined to submit to no undelegated and consequently unlimited power, in no man, or body of men on earth — even the president, whose suspicions may be the evidence, his orders the sentence, his officers the executioner and his breast the sole record of the transaction.

"When powers are assumed which have not been delegated, a nullification of the act is the rightful remedy; and every state has a natural right in eases not within the compact, — *casus non federis* — to nullify of their own authority all assumptions of power by others within their limits.

"It would be a dangerous delusion were a confidence (in the men or our choice) to silence our fears for the safety of our rights. Confidence is everywhere the parent of despotism. Jealousy, and not confidence, prescribes limited constitutions to bind down those whom we are obliged to trust with power.

"In questions of power then, let there be no more heard of confidence in man; but bind him down from mischief by the chains of the constitution."

Had Abraham Lincoln heeded these great truths, there would have been no War between the States.

Partisan books, labeled *History*, have taught false theories until their practice has obtained, in press and pulpit, to a dangerous extent. The truth is not always comfortable; but, it is always safe.

A few days ago some of my old veteran comrades cheered the sentiment that "Washington, Jefferson, Lincoln, *et al, established and defended Democratic principles.*"

My veneration for Washington isolates him from all other men; yet, I love to think he was just human; and at times so near anti-republican centralism, that the cleavage between razed his plume — lofty as it was. Wisely he trusted Jefferson. The heritage he left to John Adams brought on the political revolution of 1798-1800, led by Jefferson and Madison, as noted.

Antagonizing those principles is dangerous.

If the Constitutional principles then established, and practiced, by Jefferson, were ever practiced or defended, by Abraham Lincoln, will not some one cite us to the time, the occasion, and the proof?

I have not found either.

My friend, the Blade, has not withered with age, nor bent to cringe and apostatize. The grip and housings are somewhat battered; but, the steel grey body is as keen, as ready, as reliable, as when it clanged at a camp fire dance, or gleamed, midst those dear "Grey Riders" when our dauntless Chieftain — Hampton — led the way! My eyes are a little dimmed, my hand less steady, my step less elastic, than when the Blade and I were "first acquaint;" but, our hearts are strangely young, and still burn as we recall those scenes lang syne.

In the night silences the Blade and I often commune, — without words, — a kind of flow of soul. In one of these reveries, a bit ago, there came, softly, musically, through the stillness — "I never shall forget the day —"

I turned to the Blade, inquiringly, and realized it was voices, of long ago, singing *Kitty Wells*. Then followed *Ben Bolt,* and *Lorena.* After a pause, *Her Bright Smile Haunts Me Still,* floated to us on *Evening Breezes,* bringing memories of a tryst with *Sweet Belle Mahone* at *Killarney,* midst *Scenes That Are Brightest;* and then, to meet *Robin Adair,* and *John Anderson My Jo, Within a Mile of Edinboro Town.*

Will the "old songs" waft the fragrance of the past to the *Grey Shades — Beyond the River?*

I hope so.

The Blade presses closer, and whispers of a clean-cut Englishman who came to us and volunteered to wear "grey." He rode with us — near the front, too — when danger was abroad.

I wonder if any others are left who remember how, in the stilly night, this quiet man, Frederick Crouch, would sing his appeal to her he loved so loyally, and pleaded to so long — *Kathleen Mavourneen?*

Across all the years I can hear Crouch voicing this — his own son, — with his whole heart in it. A talented man, whose life was shadowed by sorrow, he had few intimates; but, was a gallant "Grey Rider," and good to know. He died, at Baltimore, with *Mavourneen's* hand in his, many years ago.

In all the changes that have come since those days our

Democratic principles — the basis of that four years' struggle, — have remained unchanged, steadfast. Our experience in the Greely episode taught us that a Democrat — in spirit, and in truth — cannot always follow the vagaries of the party.

As I now write — 1917 — I am oppressed by the fact that the party has "lost its tag;" abandoned its basic principles; swallowed Hamilton's whole creed and practice; established military autocracy to an unknown limit; forgotten Washington's and Jefferson's advice and warnings; and, is off again to a funeral!

The Blade soothingly assures me, "Principles don't have funerals. We are safe while we keep a sure grip on our principles."

Recently the Blade and I were discussing these topics and I read aloud that "The Civil War began when Fort Sumter was fired on by the South."

Instantly the Blade was alert; there was a sound of steely friction.

Then I read an extract from Abraham Lincoln's message to Congress, December 1864, and emphasized this sentence:

"I simply mean to say that the war will cease, on the part of the government, whenever it shall cease on the part of those who began it."

"What's that?" The metallic ring of the restless Blade was ominous.

"Why, the United States Government and Abraham Lincoln began the war by committing at least four flagrant acts of war, against two vital points in the South, weeks before Fort Sumter was fired on. That these acts were secret, and the most treacherous known to civilized diplomacy, does not weaken the force of the facts. The secrecy emphasizes the treachery.

"Had secret orders been obeyed, or other like orders not miscarried, war would have been openly inaugurated at a point 500 miles from Fort Sumter, long before Fort Sumter was fired on.

"That the first open clash was at Fort Sumter, was an accident, caused by a misfit in Abraham Lincoln's schemes to force war 'at any risk or cost.'"

I reminded the Blade. There was a solemn agreement, an armistice, existing at Charleston, entered into by the United States government and South Carolina officials on December 6, 1860; and a special agreement, armistice, at Pensacola, entered into by the United States and Florida authorities on January 29, 1861 — (both filed in United States War and Navy Departments) — by which the United States agreed not to attempt to reinforce Major Anderson, nor Fort Pickens; and South Carolina, Florida and the Confederate authorities, agreed to make no attack on Major Anderson or Fort Pickens, while these solemn agreements were observed.

To violate an armistice is considered a treacherous act of war.

For either party to prepare to act against a point covered by an armistice, is an act of war. It has been held, and rightly, that for any person to visit a fortification, where an armistice exists, with the intent to advise or plan means or methods, to strengthen such fortification is the act of a spy, a reinforcement, and an act of war.

The first who renders force necessary to defend and protect a right, is the "aggressor" in a war.

So that any act, any order intended to change the existing *status quo* at any vital point, especially where an armistice exists, by strengthening, or arranging to strengthen, such a place, thus making force necessary, is a treacherous act of war.

Yet, you say that the United States government, and Abraham Lincoln, ordered, and secretly organized and sent, armed expeditions, under *secret* instructions, to commit acts in violation of existing armistices.

Why to organize such a force, to mobilize it, for such a purpose, is an act of war. Where an armistice exists, such an order is a flagrant act of war.

You are making very serious charges, my friend.

The Blade firmly rejoined:

"I am stating facts, incontrovertible truths, and I am citing them from secret places, to establish who began war.

"If the facts establish who was innocent, don't worry about

the guilty, for the Prince of Darkness cares for his own —
makes them 'angels' in his torrid country. In our country we
honor them in monumental stone, and send them, in 'bronze,'
to teach foreign nations — especially Russia — how to obtain
and preserve Liberty!"

Again I reminded the Blade:

History does not state these "facts" as you do.

The Blade flashed back:

"History doesn't have to tell the truth; I wish it did; it
would prevent an enormous waste of sentiment in this country.
Much of this sentiment is so ignorant, hysterical, blind, that
it often antagonizes truth. Some of us remember its suppress-
ing books because they contained the truth, or even a truthful
quotation.

Why was Lamon's *Life of Lincoln* so suppressed?

"Dr. A. T. Bledsoe noticed it at length in the old *Southern
Quarterly Review*. Was its truth its crime ?

"Ward H. Lamon knew Lincoln, was his law partner.
Lincoln made him a colonel in the Secret Service, and he was
active in the events I am noting. Evidently Lincoln trusted
Lamon; used Lamon. Why, and by whom, was Lamon suppressed — later?

"When Mr. Davis, Mr. Stephens, Generals 'Dick' Taylor,
Dabney, Maury, Admiral Seinmes and others wrote defenses
of the South, many vital, illuminating facts were not available.
They charged deceit and treachery ; but it was denied, scoff-
ingly.

"Mr. Stephens weakened his charges by making personal
excuses for Lincoln. My Bible teaches that the personal accom-
plishments of the fallen Lucifer enable him to lead us to the
regions below. A man's liberty is very like his religion, both free
to all; but only at the price of 'Eternal vigilance.'

"The truth must be preserved by constant care. Falsehood
fattens on the public common.

"I repeat, the United States government committed an act
of war within eight days after Lincoln was inaugurated, with
approval of Lincoln; and, this same day, Lincoln, personally,

committed an act clearly demonstrating his intent and purpose to bring on war.

"Bear in mind that Captain Vogdes, U.S. Army, was sent with an armed force, on the U.S.S. *Brooklyn*, to reinforce Fort Pickens in January 1861; but was estopped by the 'armistice' of January 29th, at Pensacola bar; and that this armed force remained there, under Captain Vogdes, on the *Brooklyn*.

"As soon as Lincoln became president and commander-in-chief, these facts became known to him officially; and the following order was sent to violate the existing armistice, reinforce Fort Pickens, and inaugurate war. It is well known that General Scott was opposed to war; but he obeyed the Commander-in-Chief Abraham Lincoln. I quote the record.

(Extract)

"Hd. Qrs. of the Army,
"Washington, March 12th, 1861.

"Sir:

(C) At the first favorable opportunity, you will land your company, reinforce Fort Pickens, and hold the same till further orders, etc.

By command of Lieut. Gen. Scott.

(Signed) E. D. TOWNSEND,
Asst. Adjt. Gen.

To Captain I. Vogdes,
First Artillery, U.S. Army,
on board Ship of War *Brooklyn*,
off Fort Pickens,
Pensacola, Fla."

"This order was sent by U.S.S. *Crusader*, and received by Captain Vogdes, off Pensacola, on March 31, 1861. The next morning he sent to Captain H. A. Adams, the following :

"Off Pensaeola, Fla.
April 1st, 1861.

"Sir:

(D) Herewith I send you a copy of an order received by me last night. You will see by it that I am directed to land my command at the earliest opportunity. I have therefore to request that you will place at my disposal such boats and other means as will enable me to carry into effect the enclosed order.

(Signed) I. VOGDES,
Capt. 1st Artly. Comdg.

To Captain H. A. Adam,
Commanding Naval Forces off Pensaeola."

"Captain Adams averted open war on April 1, 1861, by refusing to obey this order.

"In his report to the Secretary of the Navy, Captain Adams says:

(E) "It would be considered not only a declaration but an act of war; and would be resisted to the utmost.

"Both sides are faithfully observing the agreement (armistice) entered into by the United States government and Mr. Mallory and Colonel Chase, which binds us not to reinforce Fort Pickens unless it shall be attacked or threatened. It binds them not to attack it unless we should attempt to reinforce it."

Upon receipt of this precise "Report" from Captain Adams, the secretary of the navy, regardless of the existing armistice, sent the following, (note its secrecy) :

"Navy Dept., April 6th, 1861.
"(Confidential).
Sir:

(F) Your dispatch of April 1st is received. The Department regrets that you did not comply with the request of Capt. Vogdes. You will immediately on the first favorable opportunity after receipt of this order, afford every facility to Capt. Vogdes to enable him to land the troops under his command, it being the wish and intention of the Navy Department to cooperate with the War Department, in that object.

(Signed) GIDEON WELLES,
Secty. of the Navy.

To Captain H. A. Adams,
Commanding Naval Forces off Pensacola."

(G) "This order was sent by a special messenger, Lieut. J. L. Worden, U.S.N. Worden went by rail, via Richmond, Augusta, Atlanta (Georgia); when near Atlanta he became alarmed from

Truth of the War Conspiracy of 1861

some cause, and he opened the dispatches, committed them to memory; then destroyed them; (the act of a spy.) He arrived at Pensacola at midnight, April 10th.

"On 11th of April Worden saw General Bragg, and assured General Bragg that he 'only had a verbal message of a pacific nature for Captain Adams.'

"The lieutenant was allowed to go out to Captain Adams, under this 'pacific' assurance, and the existing 'armistice.'

"Rough weather prevented Worden from reaching Captain Adams on the 11th. (It also prevented open war on April 11, 1861, by delaying Worden.)

"On April 12th Worden delivered, 'verbally, from memory, the order to reinforce Fort Pickens.

"Worden returned to Pensacola about 5:30 P.M., April 12th. He avoided seeing General Bragg and boarded a train for Montgomery, en route back to Washington.

(J) "Worden's actions aroused suspicion, and he was followed and arrested next morning at Montgomery. By some means he escaped a spy's fate and was held as a prisoner of war.

"About a year later Worden commanded the iron clad *Monitor* in her fight with the C.S.S. *Virginia* (*Merrimac*).

(K) "To avoid a spy's fate Worden made a statement, April 16, 1861 to L. P. Walker, Confederate States Secretary of War.

(H) "On April 14th General Bragg reported his experience with Worden.

(G) "It was not until four years later, September, 1865, (when the war was over, and the spy safe) that Worden reported these facts to the U.S. Navy Department. This report proves his statement to Secretary Walker to have been a tissue of lies.

(L) "Captain Adams reported having landed Vogdes, and reinforced Fort Pickens, on April 12th; but, the fact is, that Vogdes, impatient of delay, actually landed a part of his armed force and reinforced Fort Pickens after 9 P.M. on the night of April 14, 1861. Here is my authority:

(M) "April 11th at 9 P.M. the *Brooklyn* got under way and stood in toward the harbor; and during the night landed troops and marines on board, to reinforce Fort Pickens.'

"That is from the official Log of a U.S. Ship of War, as reported to, and filed in, the U.S. Navy Department. It confirms Vogdes' statement at Fort Adams.

"Captain Adams averted open war by refusing to obey orders twelve days before Fort Sumter was fired on.

"Captain Vogdes committed an act of war at Fort Pickens, the night before Sumter was fired on.

"The instant that order was issued, March 12, 1861, War was inaugurated, just one month before Sumter was fired on.

"The instant a military order is issued the whole power of the government enforces it.

"The intent was to use this power to force the South to submit to Lincoln's unconstitutional theories and acts, (confessed so, by Lincoln himself; and, held so, by Congress) or, defend our rights.

"That order inaugurated war inevitably. A sense of honor in a naval officer averted open war twelve days before Sumter was summoned to surrender. For this, this officer was officially reproved, and a special, secret, confidential order was sent to him by a spy messenger, to obey the original order, (of March 12, 1861), 'that object being the wish and intention.'

"This shows that on March 12, 1861, when that order was issued, it was the 'wish and intention' of the U.S. government to begin war.

"There is no possible escape from this.

"The official record proves it.

"In addition to this. Captain Adams obeyed the secret spy's orders, and inaugurated open war at Fort Pickens, on April 12, 1861, the same day Sumter was fired on 500 miles away; and it was more than a week 'before it was known at either fort what had occurred at the other. The treacherous collusion was secretly held in Abraham Lincoln's 'yearning' mind."

The Blade paused, and I interposed:

Do you mean that all this was done secretly, while the Confederate Peace Commission was kept waiting? (being deceived by Seward and Lincoln.)

(N) "Why, Seward assured them, through Judge Campbell, on March 15th, that "Sumter will be evacuated in ten days;" and, there "is no intent to reinforce Fort Sumter." This assurance was repeated on March 20th; Seward pleading for time and alleging that certain men were urging the government to use force; and that time was necessary to enable the government to overcome this demand for force, and make a peaceable settlement. Seward also assured Judge Campbell "as to Fort Pickens, he, (Judge Campbell), should have notice of any design to alter the existing status there."

I am quoting Judges John A. Campbell, and Samuel Nelson, of the U.S. Supreme Court, who were both present at all these interviews; and, whose veracity, unlike Seward's, has never been questioned.

You know the Confederate States Peace Commissioners presented their request on March 12, 1861; the very day you say the order was sent to "reinforce Fort Pickens."

The Blade pressed in.

(O) "Yes; and on that same day, March 12, 1861, (through one of his Cabinet, Montgomery Blair), telegraphed to Blair's kinsman, G. V. Fox, to come to Washington to arrange for an expedition to reinforce Fort Sumter.

"These facts prove two other facts.

"First: 'That the South was diligently using every means possible to preserve and establish peace; and used no treachery.

"Second: That the United States government, and Abraham Lincoln, deceived the people; deceived Congress, deceived the Confederate States Commissioners, by hypocritical 'yearnings,' and private, confidential and secret official acts, all done to insure Lincoln's scheme to force war on the South.

"On March 15, 1861, Senator Stephen A. Douglas introduced a resolution in the U.S. Senate 'To withdraw all U.S. forces from the forts in the seceded states, except at Key West and Tortugus' (which were isolated, and really international in scope.)

"Mr. Douglas also made a strong plea for peace and justice; and he clearly defined the limit of the president's powers.

"Senators Clingham and Breckenridge introduced like

resolutions; but the Senate adjourned March 28th, without action on either resolution.

"Does any man believe this Senate would have 'adjourned' if it had even suspicions of Lincoln's secret treachery? The Senate was deceived by the hypocrisy of the conspirators, led by Lincoln and Seward.

"Of this action and its effect Mr. Stephens says (Vol. II, 354):

"'But the understanding in the city (Washington), at the time of Mr. Douglas' speech, and the time the assurance was given to the Confederate States Commissioners was, that Fort Sumter was to be immediately evacuated.

"'This intelligence was telegraphed throughout the country on the 14th of March; the second day after the date of the Confederate States Commissioners' note to Mr. Seward, and the day before the first meeting Mr. Seward had with Judge Campbell. I have little doubt, therefore, that, at that time, Mr. Lincoln had decided to withdraw all United States forces from the limits of the Confederate States.'

"No man believes that General Scott ordered Captain Vogdes to commit an act of war without the order or the approval of the Commander-in-Chief Abraham Lincoln; for, it was known General Scott was opposed to war, and advised against it. General Scott's words were: 'Let the wayward sisters go in peace.'

"That order emanated from Abraham Lincoln. No other power could have forced it. General Scott obeyed orders.

"Mr. Stephens wrote in ignorance of the fact that Lincoln had secretly committed an act of war the very day the Confederate Peace Commissioners presented their peace proposal, March 12, 1861, a week after Lincoln was inaugurated, and three days before Mr. Douglas introduced his resolution.

"Another fact is here established; that the first move by each party was on March 12, 1861. The South comes for peace openly; and Lincoln comes with a war order — in secret!

"Had Lincoln died a natural death, that 'cunning which was genius,' would have destroyed the evidence of his secret, private, confidential, treacherous acts of war, which he covered up by complaining of his soul being 'burdened,' and his heart 'yearning for peace and union,' while he secretly, viciously, remorselessly inaugurated the war against the South!

"If the God of our fathers, through the tragedy of Lincoln's death, saved the truth for us and posterity, let us remember that better men than Abraham Lincoln have died that truth might live.

"I have found no record, no authority, showing that Abraham Lincoln ever entertained a 'peaceful intent' except in his own protestations; which the facts, as to his own acts, prove to have been utterly false; and intended to deceive and mislead.

(O) "In 1865 G. V. Fox made a detailed report as to his expedition.

(P) "In a letter to Montgomery Blair, dated March 1, 1861, Fox says pointedly, that the object of his plans was 'the reinforcing of Fort Sumter.' In his detailed statement (1865) he says on February 6, (1861) I met, by arrangement (at Army Headquarters) Lieutenant Norman J. Hall, who had been sent from Fort Sumter by Major Anderson' and 'we discussed the question of relieving Fort Sumter. 'Lieutenant Hall's plan' was discussed. So, Hall, whom Anderson sent, had a plan.

(R) On March 8, 1861, Fox writes to General Scott: 'Lieutenant Hall and myself have had several free conferences; and, if he is permitted by South Carolina authorities to re-enter Fort Sumter, Major Anderson will comprehend the plan for his relief.'

"This can only mean that Anderson was in collusion with Fox, Hall, Blair, Lincoln and others in their plans to 'reinforce Sumter' and inaugurate war; for Hall was 'sent by Major Anderson' and met and conferred with Fox 'by arrangement;' and was intending, if 'permitted,' to 're-enter Fort Sumter,' and naturally report to Major Anderson who would 'comprehend the plan' to 'reenforce and relieve Fort Sumter.'

(S) "Remember that Major Anderson commanded Fort Moultrie with its garrison when South Carolina seceded December 20, 1860. On December 26th, the country was electrified by the news that 'during the previous night, Major Anderson had dismantled Fort Moultrie, spiked his guns, burned his gun carriages, and removed his command to Fort Sumter.'

"Up to that time South Carolina had not seized a fort. This action violated the agreement not to change the existing military status; and South Carolina at once took possession of the other forts and defenses.

"Anderson was now scheming with Fox, Blair, Hall, and Lincoln on a 'plan' to reinforce Sumter.

Every one of them knew it meant war. Not a word, not an act, in the whole plans could be twisted into a 'yearning for peace and union.'

(O) "G. V. Fox arrived at Washington on March 13th and had several interviews with Lincoln, Blair and General Scott. It appears that General Scott still opposed any forcing of war.

"On March 19th Fox at his own suggestion, was sent to Fort Sumter where he had an interview with Major Anderson the 21st, and arranged for Anderson to hold out until 'April 15th.' Fox then returned to Washington, made his report, and the expedition took shape. So that Fox was simply Lincoln's spy and his arrangement with Anderson (which Fox denies, but facts sustain) was, and was intended to be, a 'reinforcement.'

"The U.S. Senate was in executive session; but no mention of these secret matters was made to this Senate (or any other), by Lincoln. Postmaster General Blair was the active supporter of the Lincoln-Fox war expedition.

"Montgomery Blair was a West Point graduate, and ex-officer of the U.S. Army, who left the service to practice law. He was counsel for Dred Scott in the noted case before the U.S. Supreme Court; and was now urging the Fox expedition, knowing it meant war.

"On March 28th the Senate adjourned. The next day Lincoln began to act, and sent the following order to the Secretary of the Navy:

"Executive Mansion,
March 29th, 1861.

"Sir:

(T) I desire that an expedition, to move by sea be got ready to sail as early as the 6th of April next, the whole according to memorandum attached: and that you cooperate with the Secretary of War for that object.

Your obedient servant,
(Signed) A. LINCOLN.

"To Honorable Secretary of the Navy."

"The memorandum attached called for — from the Navy — three ships of war. The *Pocahontas*, the *Pawnee* and the *Harriet Lane*; and '300 seamen, and one month's stores.' From the War Department '200 men, ready to leave garrison; and one year's stores.'

(O) " On March 30th Lincoln sent G. V. Fox to New York to prepare transports, etc., for the Fort Sumter expedition; and the (V) Secretary of the Navy issued orders, marked 'private' for the three ships of war, named by Lincoln, to be ready by April 6th."

Again I questioned the Blade:

(N) Have you forgotten that on Saturday, March 30th, Judge Campbell, who was the intermediary selected by Secretary Seward to communicate between Lincoln, Seward and the Confederate States Commissioners, saw Mr. Seward about a telegram from Governor Pickens (of South Carolina), making inquiries as to rumors about Fort Sumter; and that Seward reassured Judge Campbell, and promised "a satisfactory answer to the governor's telegram by next Monday, April 1st?"

This telegram from Governor Pickens inquired concerning Colonel Lamon, who was in Charleston, "ostensibly to arrange the proposed evacuation of Fort Sumter."

On Monday, April 1st, Mr. Seward stated to Judge Campbell, "The president may desire to supply Fort Sumter but will not do so;" and added, "There is no design to reinforce Fort Sumter."

Do you mean to say that in the face of these official,

peaceful assurances, which held the Confederates Commission waiting; that these war expeditions were secretly ordered, and organized by Lincoln and Seward, to reinforce Fort Pickens and Fort Sumter? Why that was actual, active war!

The Blade responded pointedly:

"Yes! I mean to say that; and more. Remember that Seward and Shouler both clearly state that Lincoln was privy to all of Seward's actions. April 1, 1861, was a very red letter day for what Seward described as that 'cunning which was genius' in Abraham Lincoln.

The following order by General Scott varies the usual military form so as to place the responsibility on higher authority. The first sentence clearly indicates this to any one conversant with military affairs. Lincoln's written approval fastens the fact.

(Extracts)   "Hd. Qurs. of the Army,
                                          Washington, April 1st, 1861.
"Sir:

(W) You have been designated to take command of an expedition to reinforce and hold Fort Pickens in the harbor of Pensacola. You will proceed to New York where steam transportation for four companies will be engaged; — and putting on board such supplies as you can ship without delay proceed at once to your destination. The object and destination of this expedition will he communicated to no one to whom it is not already known.

                              (Signed) WINFIELD SCOTT.
To Brevet Colonel Harvey Brown, U.S. Army.
Approved April 2, 1861.

                         "(Signed) ABRAHAM LINCOLN."

"Evidently General Scott required Lincoln's written authority before committing this act of war.

"Lincoln, to insure the intent of this order, issued a special order, as follows:

                              (Enclosure) "Executive Mansion,
                                          Washington, April 1, 1861.
(X) "All officers of the Army and Navy, to whom this

order may be exhibited will aid by every means in their power the expedition under the command of Colonel Brown; supply him with men and material; and cooperating with him as he may desire.

(Signed) ABRAHAM LINCOLN."

The Blade paused and I remarked:

You have cited two expeditions to "reinforce Fort Pickens" — Vogdes and Brown; and the Fox expedition to "reinforce Fort Sumter."

(N) Yet, that same day, April 1, 1861, Seward had solemnly assured Judge Campbell that he should have notice of any design to change the "existing status at Fort Pickens" and reasserted there was "no design to reinforce Fort Sumter."

The Blade resumed:

"Well, Seward had his part in the Lincoln scheme and played it; just as Chase did in the Peace Congress. It was all in keeping with Lincoln's creed and practice.

"In 1848 Lincoln was an avowed 'Revolutionist.' In 1858, after seventy years of phenomenal growth and prosperity, he declared 'this government cannot continue to exist half slave and half free."

"That was a good anti-constitutional 'Revolutionist' text.

"In December 1860, Senator Douglas introduced in the U.S. Senate a measure to protect the states in their constitutional rights; and to punish those guilty of interstate insurrection or invasions such as John Brown's Harper's Ferry murder and arson raid.

"In a speech at Cooper Union, New York, Lincoln denounced this Douglas Resolution, or measure, as a 'Sedition Bill.' Was not that protecting and defending John Brown's raid of arson and murder; and such like crimes against society and government? If so, how will you designate such a character?

"Fort Sumter will be supplied, peaceably if allowed, forcibly if necessary.

"Considered as an incident, (Lincoln being elected but not yet inaugurated), it suggests that perhaps such a measure as Senator Douglas introduced would have hampered Lincoln's secret designs.

"I have alluded to the public announcement by S.P. Chase, Lincoln's avowed spokesman, in the 'Peace Congress' in 1861; thirty days before Lincoln was inaugurated.

(xx)"That was the most open, direct, defiant, disunion speech ever made by a representative of any party in the United States, to that date, outside of New England. Radicals, like Thad Stevens, paralleled it later.

"It asserted, unequivocally, that the election of 1860 empowered Lincoln's party to enforce their political theories on the country, regardless of the Constitution, the laws, the rights of the states, or the decisions of the Supreme Court; and that Lincoln would do so.

"And he did.

(Y) "Five days before Lincoln was inaugurated Congress passed a resolution pronouncing the practice of political theories (as promulgated by S.P. Chase and several Northern states), to be violations of the Constitution.

"The new Congress (elected in 1860), was more favorable to the constitution being upheld than was the outgoing Congress, which passed the resolution cited; and knowing this, Lincoln did not convene this Congress until war was actually assured."

I questioned the Blade:

"That being true, as you state, what of Lincoln's 'yearning for peace and union,' which so 'burdened his soul?' You would put him in the class with John Brown.

After a moment the Blade answered:

"I have no desire to insult John Brown. I am citing facts, in the interest of justice and truth. If these facts indicate that Lincoln was an enlarged edition of the Harper's Ferry anarchist, these same *facts make the inference to remit from Lincoln's own actions.*

"If Lincoln 'yearned' for peace, why did he refuse to even discuss peace with the Peace Commissioners who were there in Washington, deceived and waiting?

"If 'peace and union burdened' his soul, why did he not

convene Congress to assume the 'burden' of peace, or war, as the Constitution required?

"Have you forgotten Lincoln's attack on the Virginia Convention? This sovereign convention met at Richmond February 13, 1861. It voted down several secession resolutions about three to one. It was for the Constitutional Union.

(Z) "This convention remained in session waiting impatiently for Lincoln to put into actual practice his avowed 'peace and union' intent and purpose; but this convention was also on guard; ready to protect Virginia from any unconstitutional acts. Lincoln's consciousness of his own secret perfidy made him fear this convention; and he attempted to have it dissolved, so as to leave Virginia open to his schemes, a la Maryland.

"On April 2, 1861, the very day he had approved a secret act of war, i.e., to 'reinforce Fort Pickens,' Lincoln and Seward selected — as Lincoln's confidential messenger — a gentleman, a Virginian, a constitutional union man, then practicing law in Washington; and at that time Judge Advocate of the U.S. Naval Court Martial. This was Allan B. Magruder.

"Lincoln instructed Magruder to go to Richmond, see Judge George W. Summers (a leading union member of the Virginia Convention, one of the five delegates to the 'Peace Congress') and urge Summers to 'come to Washington, at once, by next Friday' to confer with Lincoln on 'matters of great importance,' and if Summers could not come, then for Summers to 'select a union man to come.'

"Magruder went to Richmond that night (Tuesday, April 2nd). He saw Judge Summers, who, being unable to leave Richmond, consulted other union men, and they selected and sent John B. Baldwin, a fellow member, union man, to 'confer with Lincoln.'

"Baldwin was in secret conference with Lincoln, Thursday morning, April 4th. Baldwin advised, urged Lincoln to call a conference of the states, and to issue a 'peaceful union proclamation,' giving official assurance of what Lincoln had so broadly preached of 'yearning for peace.'

"Lincoln said, 'I fear you are too late.' *Lincoln knew he then had four secret war expeditions moving.*

"Lincoln appealed to Baldwin:

"'Why don't you adjourn the convention? Yes, I mean *sine die*. It is a standing menace to me.'

"Lincoln was afraid of that convention.

"Baldwin refused to have the convention adjourned, and warned Lincoln: 'If a gun is fired, Virginia will secede in 48 hours.'

"Baldwin could get no assurance from Lincoln, whose object was to adjourn that convention.

"As Baldwin left, he met, and spoke to, 'Seven Governors' waiting in Lincoln's rooms.

"This is the only authentic statement I have seen of these mysterious 'Seven Governors' who were credited with urging Lincoln to 'use force.'

"Lincoln had made the war inevitable, before this meeting.

"Ten days later, after three of Lincoln's secret and treacherous acts had culminated in open war, this colossal 'yearning' hypocrite 'proclaimed' war, and gave as his excuse that the South fired on Fort Sumter. He also called Congress to meet in special session; but 'cunningly' postponed its assembling eighty days to July 4, 1861.

"He could have convened Congress in ten days. He did convene an army at Washington, in less than ten days. To convene Congress in ten days would have hampered Lincoln's schemes.

"That Virginia Convention had not adjourned and that union convention voted to secede, 88 to 55, 'within 48 hours,' as Colonel Baldwin had warned; Baldwan and Summers both voting for secession.

"As to Seward, and his assurances to Judge Campbell, as to Fort Sumter; the following document is distinct enough to fix his treachery:

(Extracts) Hd. Qurs. of the Army,
(Confidential) Washington, April 4, 1861.

"Sir:

(1) This will be handed to you by Captain G. V. Fox, an

ex-officer of the Navy. He is charged by authority here, with the command of an expedition (under cover of certain ships of war) whose object is, to reinforce Fort Sumter.

To embark with Captain Fox, you will cause a detachment of recruits, say about 200, to be immediately organized at Fort Columbus, with competent number of officers, arms, ammunition, and subsistence, with other necessaries needed for the augmented garrison at Fort Sumter.

Consult Captain Fox, etc.

(Signed) WINFIELD SCOTT.
To Lieut. Col. H. L. Scott, Aide de Camp."

I commented again:

Why, *the official notice sent to Governor Pickens* was that "Fort Sumter will be supplied, peaceably if allowed, forcibly if necessary." *These are orders to 'reinforce* Fort Sumter.'" You are questioning the truth of this official notice.

"Exactly *that*," responded the Blade.

The Blade mused a moment, then continued:

"There is more yet of April 1st. Having three expeditions under way to reinforce Forts Pickens and Sumter, each an act of war, Lincoln decided to send a fourth expedition, to hasten, and insure war, by a direct and violent use of force.

"This expedition he planned and organized personally. In it he deceived his secretary of the navy and kept the War Department in ignorance. Even Fox never knew of it until all was over.

"For this expedition Lincoln selected Lieutenant D. D. Porter, U.S.N., and ordered him to take the fastest ship of war in the Atlantic squadron.

"Here are the orders:

"Executive Mansion,
Washington, April 1, 1861.

"Sir:

(2) You will proceed to New York and with least possible delay assume command of any steamer available.

Proceed to Pensacola Harbor, and at any cost or risk, prevent any expedition from the main land reaching Fort Pickens, or Santa Rosa.

You will exhibit this order to any Naval Officer at Pensacola, if you deem it necessary, after you have established yourself within the harbor.

This order, its object, and your destination will be communicated to no person whatever, until you reach the harbor of Pensacola.   (Signed) ABRAHAM LINCOLN.

To Lieutenant D. D. Porter, U.S. Navy.

Recommended:

(Signed) Wm. H. Seward."

"Lincoln knew there was an armistice existing at Pensacola. The narrow channel leading into the harbor was guarded by more than 100 Confederate guns.

"*This order was to violate the harbor and force a passage* into the 'harbor of Pensacola.'

It was war!

"One of the forts guarding this channel, Barrancas, was commanded by Captain Theodore O'Hara, C.S. Army.*

"On the same day Lincoln sent the following telegram:

"Washington, April 1, 1861.

(3) "Fit out *Powhatan* to go to sea at the earliest possible moment, under sealed orders. Orders by a confidential messenger go forward tomorrow.

(Signed) ABRAHAM LINCOLN.

To Commandant Navy Yard, Brooklyn, N.Y."

"The following order was also sent confirming the telegram:

"Executive Mansion,
April 1, 1861.

"Sir:

(3) You will fit out the *Powhatan* without delay. Lieutenant Porter will relieve Captain Mercer in command of her. She is bound on secret service; and you will under no circumstances

---

*Author of *Bivouac of the Dead*. Soon after this O'Hara was elected colonel of the 12th Regiment Alabama Volunteers. Later he was chief of staff to General John C. Breckenridge. The writer met him at Shiloh, knew him at Columbus and witnessed his final entombment at Frankfort.

communicate to the Navy Department the fact that she is fitting out.

(Signed) ABRAHAM LINCOLN.

To Commandant Navy Yard, New York."

(14) "The *Powhatan* had just made the run Havana to New York in five days. She could probably make New York to Pensacola in the same time.

"The signatures of these conspirators to these orders brands Abraham Lincoln's 'yearnings' as hypocritical whinings; his inaugural assurances, 'The government will not assail you,' and his statements to A.B. Magruder and John B. Baldwin as exactly characteristic.

"It brands every statement of his henchmen and co-conspirator, Seward, to which Lincoln was privy, as deliberate, willful, malicious, conspiring treachery.

"On this same day, April 1st, the Secretary of the Navy, being ignorant of Lincoln's secret orders to *Powhatan*, added the *Powhatan* to the Lincoln-Fox-Fort Sumter expedition, with her captain, Mercer, in command of the fleet, as the following shows:

"Telegram.   Washington, April 1, 1861.

(4) Fit out *Powhatan* to go to sea at earliest possible moment.

(Signed) GIDEON WELLES, Secty. of Navy.

To Commandant Navy Yard, Brooklyn, N.Y."

"It appears that the Secretary of Navy was urging the *Powhatan* to be ready for the Fox expedition against Sumter, and Lincoln was secretly hurrying the same ship for Porter to use against Pensacola.

"On April 5th the Secretary of Navy issued the following order to her Captain Mercer. He was still ignorant of Lincoln's order of April 1st:

"(Extract)

(5) "(Confidential) "Navy Dept., April 5, 1861.

"Sir:

The U.S. Steamers, *Powhatan, Pawnee, Pocahontas* and *Harriet Lane*, will compose a naval force under your command, to be sent to the vicinity of Charleston, S.C., for the purpose of aiding in carrying out the object of an expedition of which the War Department has charge. The expedition has been intrusted to Captain G. V. Fox.

You will leave New York with the *Powhatan* in time to be off Charleston bar, 10 miles distant from and due east of the lighthouse on the morning of the 11th instant, there to await the arrival of the transports with troops and stores. The *Pawnee* and *Pocahontas* will be ordered to join you there, at the time mentioned, and also the *Harriet Lane*, etc.

(Signed) GIDEON WELLES,
Secretary of Navy.

To Captain Samuel Mercer,
 Comdg. U.S.S. *Powhatan*, New York."

(6) "Regardless of this order, on April 6th, Lieut. Porter, on the *Powhatan*, sailed, under Lincoln's orders.

"Seward must have repented, lost his nerve, for he 'funked' and sent the following:

"Telegram. "April 6, 1861.

(7) "Give the *Powhatan* up to Captain Mercer.

(Signed) SEWARD.

To Lieutenant D. D. Porter."

"Porter had sailed. A dispatch boat was sent with this telegram to overtake the *Powhatan*, which it did, and Lieutenant Porter answered, as follows:

"April 6, 1861.

(8) "I received my orders from the president, and shall proceed and execute them.

(Signed) D.D. PORTER

To Hon. Wm. H. Seward."

"Before sailing on 6th, Lieutenant Porter instructed the Navy Yard officials, 'Detain all letters for five days.'

"He evidently expected to reach his destination by 'April 11.'

"Storms and defective boilers delayed the *Powhatan*, and Lieutenant Porter did not reach Pensacola at the expected time.

(9) When he arrived he had the *Powhatan* disguised and

flying English colors. Being ignorant of events at Fort Pickens (and Sumter) he headed direct for the channel, to force an entrance to Pensacola harbor. Here is what Porter himself says, in his report:

(10) "I had disguised the ship, so that she deceived those who had known her, and was standing in (unnoticed), when the *Wyandotte* commenced making signals, which I did not answer, but stood on.

The steamer then put herself in my way and Captain Meigs, who was aboard, hailed me and I stopped.

In twenty minutes more I should have been inside (Pensacola harbor) or sunk.

(Signed) D. D. PORTER, U.S. Navy."

"This action, itself, was eloquent of the design, purpose, of Lincoln's secret, specific orders to Lieutenant Porter dated April 1, 1861, to force war!

"Lincoln's 'cunning which was genius' was exemplified in the fact that he had four expeditions at the same time, to force war, at points 500 miles apart, and neither of the officers in command of an expedition knew of the existence, the object nor the destination of either of the others.

"That these secret expeditions seem to have been designed to culminate on 'the 11th instant" is a remarkably suggestive, if not indicative, coincidence.

"Rough weather, gales, storms, defective boilers, causing delays; and Adams' refusal to obey orders, all combined to make a rather tangled web of *Honest Abe's* secret treachery.

But notwithstanding all these delays and misfits, the facts establish that open war was averted on April 1, 1861, by Captain Adams, who was reproved for it; that this delayed act was accomplished by Vogdes, on the *night of April 11, 1861; before Fort Sumter was fired on (April 12, 1861.)*

"Had Fort Sumter not existed, there would have been open war forced on the South at Fort Pickens, on April 1, 1861, if Captain Adams had obeyed positive 'orders.' *That was the avowed 'wish and intention.'*"

After a moment of silence, I commented:

(12) I recall that Captain Barron of U.S. Navy, made a special report on the good faith being observed by both parties to the armistice existing at Pensaeola; and that Captain Poor, U.S. Navy, reported that the *Powhatan* attempted to force an entrance to Pensacola harbor, (9) "flying English colors."

(13) Also, that dispatches were captured, at Charleston, which divulged that Captain Fox acted the part of a spy, and so deceived Governor Pickens.

It is strange that histories and biographies do not mention these facts.

The Blade retorted:

"Histories and biographies are very much like Lincoln, who was often made to say things to fit into the designs of a powerful political faction. His first inaugural address was so doctored.

When Lincoln read that Gettysburg speech he must have wondered at his own eloquence; for he never voiced it (as printed.)

"I am not guided by what histories and biographies may say; nor by the opinions of any friend, or foe of Lincoln.

"I credit Abraham Lincoln, president of the United States, with knowing what his office required him to know, and he certainly knew. That premise fixed, his own words, and acts, are his passport — "This is Coilantogle Ford!"

"Lincoln fixed upon himself the responsibility for war, by telling only a part of the truth.

"It is significant, that he never convened Congress until July 4, 1861, months after he had the war actively inaugurated.

In his message to this Congress, he acknowledged having committed unconstitutional acts.

"The flimsy sophisms by which he attempted to excuse his usurpations would not be allowed in any court. Any school debating club would ridicule such an argument.

"Congress, dazed by war, inaugurated without its knowledge or consent, (as the constitution required), received his message July 4, 1861.

(16) "On July 10th, a joint resolution was introduced in the U.S. Senate to legalize Lincoln's unconstitutional acts. The first sentence of this 'Joint Resolution' fixes its character.

"Whereas, since the adjournment of Congress on the 4th day of March last, a formidable insurrection in certain states of this Union has arrayed itself in armed hostility to the government of the United States, constitutionally administered, etc."

"It is evident from the facts cited in this paper (which were not available for years after this resolution was penned), that there was no 'government of the United States constitutionally administered,' in existence, at the time noted. There was unconstitutional 'armed hostility' secretly organized, and sent to invade the South, while the Southern Peace Commission was in Washington urging peace; and deceived by assurances of 'peaceful intent.'

"The 'Joint Resolution' itself is based on Lincoln's acknowledgment that the 'government' was not 'constitutionally administered;' and the avowed object and intent of the 'resolution' itself was to legalize the unconstitutional administration of the 'government of the United States, by Abraham Lincoln, whose oath bound him to 'preserve, protect, and defend the Constitution of the United States.'

"Had Abraham Lincoln kept his oath and preserved the Constitution, the Union would have been preserved; and there would have been no war.

"No one knew this better than Abraham Lincoln, and his spokesman, S.P. Chase, whose defiant notice I have cited.

Lincoln made that notice good; not his oath.

"The 'Joint Resolution' names the following six unconstitutional acts, as confessed by Lincoln:

"He calls for 75,000 men, April 15, 1861.

"He proclaims a blockade, April 19, 1861.

"He proclaims a second blockade, April 27, 1861.

"He authorizes a military officer to suspend *Habeas Corpus* in Maryland and Pennsylvania, April 27, 1861.

"He calls for 35,000 volunteers, May 3, 1861.

"He authorizes a military officer to suspend *Habeas Corpus* in Florida, May 10, 1861.

"Here is the enacting clause of that 'Joint Resolution'

"'Be it resolved by the Senate and House of Representatives of the United States in Congress assembled; that all the extraordinary acts, proclamations, and orders hereinbefore mentioned be and the same are hereby approved, and declared to be in all respects legal and valid, to the same, and with the same effect as if they had been issued and done under the previous express authority, and direction, of the Congress of the United States.'

"In this enacting clause *Congress itself brands Lincoln's acts as illegal, invalid, unconstitutional.*"

Here, I interposed to say:

There is no allusion in that "Joint Resolution" to the secret, unconstitutional orders and expeditions you have cited, and which inaugurated the war, months before this Congress was allowed to convene.

Lincoln's confession begins with his proclamation April 15th. He secretly inaugurated war March 12th. He had four secret war expeditions before April 5, 1861.

Why did not Lincoln tell all the truth — to Congress?

The Blade seemed astonished by my question:

"Don't think Lincoln was a fool! He was a knave. He never told all the truth even 'part of the time.'

"He was a joker, and never knew all he told. That is why he was called 'Honest Abe.'

"To have this 'Joint Resolution' adopted by Congress, all the influence of Lincoln, his Cabinet, and his party was exerted, but, having no power to legalize crime. Congress refused.

"The 'Joint Resolution' was never even acted on to this good day!

"You may conjecture from this what would have happened if Senator Douglas had lived and been in his seat; or, if Lincoln had told 'all the truth,' (the facts as here stated), to that Congress which was opposed to the Chase doctrines.

Truth of the War Conspiracy of 1861

"Impeachment was not, in either case, an improbability.

"In 1861, Lincoln authorized a military officer to suspend the writ of *Habeas Corpus* in Pennsylvania and Maryland. "A citizen of Maryland as arrested and imprisoned in a military stronghold. The citizen sued out a writ of *Habeas Corpus.*

"Chief Justice, Roger B. Taney, of the U.S. Supreme Court, ordered the parties to appear before him at Baltimore.

"The military officer refused to supply the court with a copy of the order of arrest; and refused to obey the writ. His excuse was, that he was 'authorized by the president to suspend the writ of *Habeas Corpus* at his discretion,' and that he 'suspends it in this case.'

"Judge Taney proceeded to hear the case, *ex parte*, and rendered the court's decision.

"He pronounced every phase of the proceedings to be unconstitutional, null and void. He denied the power of the president to suspend *Habeas Corpus* under any circumstances; much less the power to authorize a military officer to exercise it.

"He ordered a copy of this decision, under the seal of the United States Supreme Court, to be delivered, by a court messenger 'to the president of the United States.'

"That was the most just and masterly rebuke ever delivered since Elijah denounced Ahab for crimes far less!

"Remember, too, that Ahab also went 'softly, yearningly,' but that 'in his son's days,' God struck!

"The venerable chief justice died during Lincoln's first term, and Lincoln appointed the constitution-defying Salmon P. Chase to succeed him.

"It is pertinent to remember, that Senator Stephen A. Douglas had pointedly declared the limit of the president's powers; and Douglas knew Lincoln. Had Mr. Douglas lived to meet with the Senate July 4, 1861, it is almost a certainty that he would have begun impeachment proceedings; but Mr. Douglas died June 3, 1861. The dying words of Mr. Douglas, to his sons were eloquent of his thought, his patriotism: 'Obey the law and support the Constitution.'

"What history or biography cites the facts as to Lincoln's attempt to buy, to bribe, the Ohio Democratic committee, when Lincoln offered to remit the sentence of Vallandingham?

"When conscription was enforced in 1863, there was a riot in New York. Among the leading men who openly denounced conscription was C. L. Vallandingham, of Ohio. General Burnside arrested Vallandingham and he was exiled, banished, by Lincoln's order.

"The Democrats of Ohio through a committee of prominent leaders petitioned Lincoln to release Vallandingham from the sentence.

(13X) "'Lincoln offered to *remit the sentence of Vallandingham, if the committee of prominent Democrats who petitioned for Vallandingham would sign a statement that rebellion existed; that Constitutional measures were taken when the army and navy were used to suppress it; and each of the committee would also use his influence and power to carry on the war.*

"The Democratic committee refused. Vallandingham was nominated by Democrats for governor of Ohio.

"Vallandingham returned, without leave, from his banishment, and was leader in Democratic Convention at Chicago, August 27-29, 1864, when McClellan was nominated.

"'Lincoln did not deem it *wise to rearrest Vallandingham.*'

"Being characteristic, comment is unnecessary.

"Much more could be said of Martial law declared; *Habeas Corpus* suspended. Legislatures throttled by military force — in non-seceding States, too — but surely this is sufficient to satisfy any open intelligence.

"G. V. Fox, the Fort Sumter spy, was made assistant secretary of the U.S. Navy. John L. Worden, the Pensacola spy, rose to be admiral.

"Who violated his official oath; violated the Constitution, and the laws; defied the Supreme Court of the United States; thus disrupting the 'Compact of Union?'

"Who suppressed the Constitutional voice of Congress, while he, secretly, with deceit and treachery, inaugurated war?

"The immutable facts answer —

"Abraham Lincoln.

"As was said of Caesar Borgia, who was Machiavelli's model: "'His genius was little more than the lack of principle, which allowed no scruple to stand in the way of his design.'

"Borgia, too, was idolized by his followers. A cardinal at 17, he convulsed his country before he was 30; was killed, in exile, at 32; and his memory and fame rest on his crimes!

"The record shows clearly there was a conspiracy led by Abraham Lincoln who was impulsed by envy and hate of the South; and whose sole ambition was to lead in destroying.

"They rioted, without scruple, in secret depths of moral and political depravity before unknown.

"No wonder that men like Mr. Jefferson Davis, Mr. Stephens, Admiral Semmes, Generals Johnston, Taylor, Maury and others hesitated to write freely; for a clean man, a gentleman, could not conceive of such depths of treachery,

"The wonder is, that such men as Lincoln, Chase, Seward, Welles, Blair, Fox, Worden, and their henchmen, with all their genius for cunning, unscrupulous depravity, failed to find one single act, or word, which could be tortured, even by their vile processes, into a tenable charge of duplicity, or crime, against the men whom the South put forward, and followed.

"THEY TRIED IT, AND FAILED!

"This knowledge is a finer heritage of truth and honor; than is advertised in all the stone, brass and bronze, from Boston to the Western sunset!"

The voice of the Blade changed ; there came a ringing, vibrating challenge in it.

"No Southern statesman; no advocate of States' Rights; ever denounced the Constitution; or the Constitutional Union;

or defied the decisions of the Supreme Court of the United States, in any speech, address, or party announcement, ever made.

"No Southern state ever failed to comply, loyally, with her obligations to every other state, or to the United States, as prescribed, and required, by the Constitution of the United States.

"I challenge refutation!"

The Blade ceased.

Do you wonder that I love the Blade for the dangers we have shared, and the unafraid Truth that is in it?

Its "Challenge" stands!

EN-AMI

To those who may resent the thrusts of the Blade:

I assert that the South did a lion's share to win the American Revolution. This, my friends, is *our* country.

We fought for it when blood was its price. We paid for its institutions when gold was the price.

Beside the Blade, a brace of fine old pistols rest, bearing many scars of service in that Revolution. In virtue of one I can wear the *Eagle* of the Cincinnati; of the other the *Southern Cross*. One typifies victory for — the other suppression of — the same principles and rights.

Principles abide!

Try and realize, my friends, that no individual is necessary to our security or our happiness; and, that the most irritating burden to a proud people is injustice; and that injustice to the right — the patriotism of a courageous people — is to them the most hideous.

When a jury of our peers consider the facts and so find one guilty — do we expect or hear denunciation of the facts, or the verdict? Is not every good citizen earnest and diligent to support justice and right?

If this is true in our communities, our States, why not so feel, so act, in this greater matter?

I may regret the necessity, but, neither I nor any lover of truth and justice should regret the result.

If I know myself it has been in this broad view that I have seen — and labored to bring before my countrymen — the jury: — the facts set forth in this article; and I appeal to you to so consider and so judge my work.

So, there stands before you as true a *Traitor* — as loyal a *Rebel* — as ever descended from Revolutionary loins.

H. W. JOHNSTONE
Idylwild, Ga.

June 12, 1917.

Judge Campbell's Letters

"Extracts."

"Sunday Morning, April 7, 1861.

(13) "Memorandum.

"The (Confederate Peace) Commissioners have been under anxiety and concern for two or three days by reports, that have some appearance of authority, of conversations of the president relative to Southern affairs, troops, and by the sailing of the *Atlantic*.*

"I have assured them that the government will not undertake to supply Sumter without giving notice to Governor Pickens, and that I should have notice whenever any measure changing the existing status prejudicially to the Confederate States is contemplated as respects Fort Pickens.

"I do not experience the same anxiety or concern as they express. But if I have said more than I am authorized I pray that you will advise me.

JOHN A. CAMPBELL.

This letter was addressed to Wm. H. Seward, Secretary of State. But this is left out in compiling the record, and a sentence is added — from Judge Campbell's report to the Confederate authorities as to this incident.

Mr. Seward's answer to this letter is also suppressed. That answer was: "Faith as to Sumter fully kept. Wait and see." That answer was in writing.

Why was Seward's name, as addressed, and Seward's answer left out of the record, and foreign matter inserted totally irrelevant to the question at issue?

Judge Campbell waited, and saw. Then wrote the following letter to Wm. H. Seward:

---

*The *Atlantic* carried the secret expedition under Brown against Fort Pickens.

"Washington City, Saturday, April 18, 1861.
"Sir:

(N)"On the 15th of March, ultimo, I left with Judge
Crawford, one of the Commissioners of the Confederate
States, a note in writing to the effect following:

"'I feel entire confidence that Fort Sumter will be evacuated in the next ten days, and this measure is felt as imposing
great responsibility on the Administration.
"'I feel entire confidence that no measure changing the existing status prejudicially to the Southern Confederate States, is
at present contemplated.

"'I feel entire confidence that an immediate demand for
an answer to the communication of the Commissioners will
be productive of evil and not of good. I do not believe that it
ought, at this time, to be pressed.'

"The substance of this statement I communicated to you
the same evening by letter. Five days elapsed and I called with
a telegram from General Beauregard to the effect that Sumter
was not evacuated, but that Major Anderson was at work making repairs.
"The next day, after conversing with you, I communicated
to Judge Crawford, in writing, that the failure to evacuate
Sumter was not the result of bad faith, but was attributable to
causes consistent with the intention to fulfill the engagement,
and that, as regarded Pickens, I should have notice of any
design to alter the existing status there.
"Mr. Justice Nelson was present at these conversations,
three in number, and I submitted to him each of my written communications to Judge Crawford, and informed Judge
Crawford that they had his (Judge Nelson's) sanction. I gave
you, on the 22nd of March, a substantial copy of the statement
I had made on the 15th.
"The 30th of March arrived, and at that time a telegram
came from Governor Pickens inquiring concerning Colonel

Lamon, whose visit to Charleston he supposed had a connection with the proposed evacuation of Fort Sumter. I left that with you, and was to have an answer the following Monday morning (1st of April.) On the 1st of April I received from you the statement in writing: 'I am satisfied the government will not undertake to supply Fort Sumter without giving notice to Governor P.' The words, 'I am satisfied' were for me to use as expression of confidence in the remainder of the declaration.

"The proposition as originally prepared was: 'The president may desire to supply Sumter, but will not do so," etc., and your verbal explanation was that you did not believe any such attempt would be made, and that there was no design to reinforce Sumter.

"There was a departure here from the pledges of the previous month, but, with the verbal explanation, I did not consider it a matter then to complain of. I simply stated to you that I had that assurance previously.

"On the 7th of April I addressed you a letter on the subject of the alarm that the preparations by the government had created, and asked you if the assurances I had given were well or ill founded. In respect to Sumter your reply was: 'Faith as to Sumter fully kept. Wait and see.'

"In the morning's paper I read: 'An authorized messenger from President Lincoln informed Governor Pickens and General Beauregard that provisions will be sent to Fort Sumter — peaceably, or otherwise by force.

"This was the 8th of April, at Charleston — the day following your last assurance and is the last evidence of the full faith I was invited to wait for and see. In the same paper I read that intercepted dispatches disclosed the fact that Mr. Fox, who had been allowed to visit Major Anderson, on the pledge that his purpose was pacific, employed his opportunity to devise a plan for supplying the fort by force, and that this plan had been adopted by the Washington government and was in process of execution.

"My recollection of the date of Mr. Fox's visit carries it to a day in March. I learn that he is a near connection of a member of the Cabinet.

"My connection with the Commissioners and yourself was superinduced by the conversation with Justice Nelson. He informed me of your strong disposition in favor of peace and that you were oppressed with a demand of the Commissioners of the Confederate States for a reply to their first letter, and that you desired to avoid it if possible at that time.

"I told him I might, perhaps, be of some service in arranging the difficulty. I came to your office entirely at his request, and without the knowledge of either of the (Confederate) Commissioners. Your depression was obvious to both Judge Nelson and myself. I was gratified at the character of the counsels you were desirous of pursuing, and much impressed with your observation that a civil war might be prevented by the success of my mediation. You read a letter of Mr. (Thurlow) Weed, to show how irksome and responsible the withdrawals of troops from Sumter was. A portion of my communication to Judge Crawford on the 15th of March, was founded upon these remarks, and the pledge to evacuate Sumter is less forcible than the words you employed. Those words were: 'Before this letter reaches you, (a proposed letter by me to President Davis), Sumter will have been evacuated.'

"The (Confederate) Commissioners who received those communications conclude they have been abused and overreached.

The Montgomery government holds the same opinion. The Commissioners have supposed that my communications were with you, and upon the hypothesis were prepared to arraign you before the country in connection with the president. I placed a peremptory prohibition upon this as being contrary to the terms of my communications with them. I pledged myself to them to communicate information upon what I considered as the best authority, and they were to confide in the ability of myself, aided by Judge Nelson, to determine upon the credibility of my informant.

"I think no candid man will read over what I have written, and consider for a moment what is going on at Sumter, but will agree that the equivocating conduct of the administration, as measured and interpreted in connection with these promises, is the proximate cause of the great calamity.

"I have a profound conviction that the telegrams of the 8th of April of General Beauregard, and of the 10th of April of General Walker, the Secretary of War, can be referred to nothing else than their belief that there has been systematic duplicity practiced on them through me. It is under an impressive sense of the weight of this responsibility that I submit to you these things for your explanation.

"Very respectfully,
"JOHN A. CAMPBELL,

"Associate Justice of the Supreme Court, United States.
"Hon. Wm. H. Seward,
"Secretary of State."

To this there was no answer.
A week later Judge Campbell wrote the following:

"Washington, April 20, 1861.
"Sir:
"I enclose you a letter, corresponding very nearly with one I addressed to you one week ago (13th April), to which I have not had any reply. The letter is simply one of inquiry in reference to facts concerning which, I think, I am entitled to an explanation. I have not adopted any opinion in reference to them which may not be modified by explanation; nor have I affirmed in that letter, nor do I in this, any conclusion of my own unfavorable to your integrity, in the whole transaction. All that I have said and mean to say is, that an explanation is due from you to myself.

"I will not say what I shall do in case this request is not complied with, but I am justified in saying that I shall feel at liberty to place these letters before any person who is entitled to such an explanation of myself.

"Very respectfully,
JOHN A. CAMPBELL,

Truth of the War Conspiracy of 1861

"Associate Justice of the Supreme Court, United States.
"Hon. Wm. H. Seward,
"Secretary of State."

No reply has been made to this letter, April 24, 1861.

These papers, and every paper connected with this affair, (in which Judge Campbell was the mediator selected by Seward), were filed in the Confederate States archives, and were delivered to United States authorities, to complete the record.

The motive which prompted the garbling and suppression of the complete record of this "systematic duplicity" is clearly apparent to any candid mind.

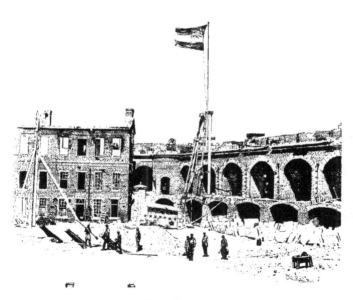

Fort Sumter

End Notes

Date of Act	Cypher	Authorities And Memoranda
1798-1832	A	Thomas Jefferson Randolph's Original Mss.
March 4, 1861	B	Lincoln's First Inaugural Address.
March 12, 1861	C	Records Rebellion, Ser. I, Vol. 4, 90. War Department to Vogdes.
April 1, 1861	D	Records Rebellion, Ser. I, Vol. 4, 110. Vogdes to Adams.
April 1, 1861	E	Records Rebellion, Ser. I, Vol 4. 109 to 114, and 125. Adams refuses to obey.
April 6, 1861	F	Records Rebellion, Ser. I, Vol. 4, 110-111. Welles Reorders Adams.
April 7-14, 1861	G	Records Rebellion. Ser. I. Vol. 4. 111. Worden's report (1865). Spy.
April 13-14, 1861	H	Records Rebellion, Ser. I, Vol. 4, 135-136. Bragg as to Worden.
April 15, 1861	J	Records Rebellion, Ser. I, Vol. 4, 118. Worden prisoner of war.
April 16, 1861	K	Records Rebellion. Ser. I, Vol. 4. 136-137. Worden to Secretary Walker. Statement.
April 12, 1861	L	Records Rebellion. Ser. I, Vol. 4. 115. Adams reports landing Vogdes.
April 11, 1861	M	Records Rebellion. Ser. I. Vol. 4. 208-209. Log of U.S.S. *Supply* night of April 11th.
March 12 to Apr. 9	N	Stephens II, Campbell-Seward letters, 743-6. Comments, 348-54.
Feb. to Apr. 12, '61	O	Records Rebellion, Vol. 4, 244-51. Fox report (1865) of Sumter Expedition.
March 1, 1861	P	Records Rebellion, Vol. 4, 225. Fox to Blair, as to "reinforcing Sumter," etc.
Feb. 8, 1861	R	Records Rebellion, Vol. 4. 223. Fox to Scott, of "Hall Conferences," etc.
December 26, 1860	S	Davis' Confederate States. 57. Anderson "Dismantles Moultrie." etc.
March 29, 1861	T	Records Rebellion. Vol. 4. 227-228. Lincoln's order. Fox "Expedition."
March 30, 1861	V	Records Rebellion. Vol. 4, 228-229. Welles' "private" orders. Ships of War.
April 1, 1861	W	Records Rebellion, Vol. 4, 107-108. Scott-Lincoln orders to Brown.
April 1, 1861	X	Records Rebellion. Vol. 4. 108. Lincoln's special orders to "all officers."
February 6, 1861	XX	Stephens, II. 43-50. Chase in "Peace Conference."

Date of Act	Cypher	Authorities And Memoranda
February 27, 1861	Y	Stephens II. 417. Resolution in Congress on Chase theories, etc.
April 2 to 4. 1861	Z	*Atlantic Monthly.* April 1875. Magruder and Baldwin, statement.
April 4, 1861	1	Records Rebellion, Vol. 4. 232-3. Gen. Scott order "Fox Expedition." Sumter.
April 1, 1861	2	Records Rebellion, Vol. 4, 108-9. Lincoln- Seward, order, to Porter.
April 1, 1861	3	Records Rebellion, Vol. 4, 109. Lincoln telegram, *Powhatan*, secret; order confirming and secret.
April 1, 186l	4	Records Rebellion, Vol. 4, 229. Welles telegram, "Fit Out' *Powhatan.*
April 5, 1861	5	Records Rebellion, Vol. 4, 235. Welles order to Mercer, *Powhatan.*
April 6, 1861	6	Records Rebellion, Vol. 4, 237-9. Porter sails; Seward's telegram.
April 6, 1861	7	Records Rebellion, Vol. 4, 112. Seward telegram to Porter, "Give up *Powhatan.*"
April 6, 1861	8	Records Rebellion, Vol. 4, 112. Porter's answer to Seward.
	9	Records Rebellion, Vol. 4. 132. Capt. Poor, "*Powhatan* flying English colors."
April 21, 1861	10	Records Rebellion, Vol. 4, 122-123. Porter's report — "20 minutes, or sunk."
April 20, 1861	11	Records Rebellion, Vol. 4, 125-128. Capt. Adams to Capt. Dupont, as to Porter, etc.
February 2, 1861	12	Records Rebellion, Vol. 4, 76-77. Capt. Barron on Armistice; also 51, Armstrong.
Apr. 7, 13, 20, 1861	13	Campbell's two letters to Seward, never answered. Stephens II, 74 3-6. Records Rebellion, Ser. I, Vol. 4, 258-259.
1863	13x	Enc. Brit, xiv., 658-61. Lincoln vs. Vallandingham.
	14	Records Rebellion, Vol. 4. 265. *Powhatan.* "Havana to New York in five days."
December 17, 1863	15	Stephens II, 49. Resolution in Congress as to "Rebels" and "Traitors."
July 10, 1861	16	Stephens II, 436. Joint Resolution to legalize Lincoln's acts, etc. The circled letters and figures on margin refer to this sheet.

Note: Records Rebellion refers to the *Official Records of the Union and Confederate Navies in the War of the Rebellion.*

Addendum

Miss Rutherford's Message

Realizing for some time that there was a mystery about the surrender of Fort Pickens and the arming and provisioning of Fort Sumter in 1861, I was delighted when Mr. Johnstone sent me his manuscript bringing to light the long concealed records, establishing beyond a doubt the truth of history.

So valuable are these proofs in placing the responsibility upon the proper person for bringing on the War Between the States that I felt it an absolute necessity to have them published.

It is impossible to right the wrongs of Southern history so long as the world believes the falsehoods published since Abraham Lincoln's assassination.

Read this pamphlet, and be honest in the reading, and be grateful to Mr. Johnstone for bringing these facts to light.

All wishing to buy copies of the pamphlet send direct to H.W. Johnston, Curryville, Ga. – Idylwild — 50 cts. per copy.

All desiring copies for the Essay Contest send direct to me — Athens, Ga. 10 cts. a copy.

Mildred Lewis Rutherford
State Historian UDC
Athens, Georgia
1921

⬿ H. W. Johnstone ⬾

Huger W. Johnstone was born in Georgia on June 12, 1844. He married Emma Olivia on November 22, 1871, in Spalding County, Georgia. She was born on April 7, 1851, also in Georgia. He died on June 23, 1924, in College Park, Fulton County, Georgia. When he enlisted as a musician on May 10, 1861, in Co. B, 5th Regiment Georgia Volunteer Infantry "Griffin Light Guards" he was living in Spalding County. He would serve until he was discharged due to disability in Chattanooga, Tennessee, on April 5, 1862.

Being true to the Cause, he would re-enlist on May 15, 1862, as a private in Co. C, 21st Battalion Georgia Cavalry which would later become Co. B, 7th Regiment Georgia Cavalry. He was wounded on August 4, 1864. His pension stated he surrendered at Appomattox Court House. His wife would receive a widow's pension until her death in Fulton County, Georgia on October 12, 1938.

Huger or H. W. is sometimes listed as Johnson or Johnston. Having ancestors who served in the Revolutionary War, he traced his ancestry to Scotland in the 1300s.

— *Charles Kelly Barrow*
August 2012